INVASION ALERT!

INVASION OF THE ASIAN CARP

DEVON PATRICK

Enslow PUBLISHING

Please visit our website, www.enslow.com. For a free color catalog of all our high-quality books, call toll free 1-800-398-2504 or fax 1-877-980-4454

Published in 2027 by
Enslow Publishing
2544 Clinton Street
Buffalo, NY 14224

Portions of this work were originally authored by Santana Hunt and published as *Animal Invaders: Destroying Native Habitats: Attack of the Asian Carp*. All new material in this edition is authored by Devon Patrick.

Cataloging-in-Publication Data
Names: Patrick, Devon.
Title: Invasion of the Asian carp / Devon Patrick.
Description: Buffalo, NY : Enslow Publishing, 2027. | Series: Invasion alert! | Includes glossary and index.
Identifiers: ISBN 9781978548305 (pbk.) | ISBN 9781978548312 (library bound) | ISBN 9781978548329 (ebook)
Subjects: LCSH: Carp--Juvenile literature. | Introduced fishes--Juvenile literature.
Classification: LCC QL638.C94 D486 2027 | DDC 597.482--dc23

Printed in China

Photos Credits: Cover, p. 1 Frantisek Czanner/Shutterstock.com; cover, p. 1, 3, 4, 6, 8, 10, 12, 14, 16, 18, 20, 22, 23, 24 (dot pattern) Nurin Nabila A/Shutterstock.com; p. 4, 6, 8, 10, 12, 14, 16, 18, 20 (sidebar frame) HST6/Shutterstock.com; p. 5 USFWS; p. 7 Dan Thornberg/Shutterstock.com; p. 9 benny337/Shutterstock.com; p. 11 Kristen Peters/USFWS; p. 13 K Steve Cope/Shutterstock.com; p. 15 SandmanPhotography/Shutterstock.com; p. 17 Ryan Hagerty/USFWS; p. 19 USGS; p. 21 Tinawww/Shutterstock.com

CPSIA compliance information: Batch #QSENS27: For further information, contact Enslow Publishing, New York, New York, at 1-800-398-2504.

CONTENTS

Words in the glossary appear in **bold** type the first time they are used in the text.

JUMPING FISH!

Imagine that you're enjoying a relaxing day of fishing on a lake ... until a huge fish leaps out of the water and into your boat! Boat motors and other loud sounds can **startle** fish. When that happens, some Asian carp can jump up to 10 feet (3 m) in the air!

Asian carp have been raised in Asia for more than 1,000 years. They were brought to North America in the 1960s and have been making their homes in U.S. waterways ever since.

STAY ALERT

Invasive species are nonnative species that are introduced to a new environment. They can be harmful to native animals and plants when put into a new **habitat**.

Silver carp can leap out of the water to escape threats. These fish are so large they can injure boaters and water skiers.

SPREADING OUT

In the 1960s and 1970s, catfish farmers brought Asian carp to the southern United States. The fish were meant to stop the growth of harmful plants, **algae**, and other pests in fish farms, ponds, and lakes.

However, some Asian carp escaped when floods raised the water levels in the lakes and ponds. The fish could then swim—or jump—into waterways that led to the Mississippi River. This large river flows into several other rivers throughout the country. The Asian carp spread quickly.

STAY ALERT

"Asian carp" is a general name for several species, or kinds, of carp that are native to China, Russia, and other parts of eastern Asia.

More than 1 million miles (1.6 million km) of rivers and streams flow into the Mississippi River. Asian carp could travel almost anywhere!

FOUR SPECIES

Asian carp in the United States include the grass carp, black carp, bighead carp, and silver carp. The different species can vary in size, but most of them are quite large. Bighead carp can be about 5 feet (1.5 m) long and grow to be more than 100 pounds (45 kg)! Grass carp can grow to be almost as big.

Silver carp and black carp are a bit smaller, weighing only about 60 to 70 pounds (27 to 32 kg). Asian carp are a silvery color, though each species' body looks a little different.

STAY ALERT

Bighead and silver carp eat **plankton**. Black carp eat snails and mussels.

Asian carp are big fish and big eaters. The grass carp can eat up to 40 percent of its body weight in plants each day. That's about 40 pounds (18 kg) of plants!

ASIAN CARP TAKEOVER

Asian carp **reproduce** by laying eggs. A female Asian carp lays eggs a few times a year. Each time, she may lay hundreds of thousands of eggs! Adult carp like to live in slow-moving water, but they move to fast-moving water to **spawn**. This allows the eggs to spread quickly.

While not all the **larvae** that hatch from these eggs will live to be adults, Asian carp still reproduce at a much higher rate than native fish. These hardy fish grow quickly.

STAY ALERT

It's hard to know how many Asian carp there are. Nets used to catch fish for counting often aren't strong enough to hold them!

Asian carp don't have many predators in North American waterways. There's nothing in their new habitat to keep their populations in check.

NOT ENOUGH FOOD

Big populations of big fish with big **appetites** can cause—you guessed it!—big problems. Of the four species of Asian carp, the silver and bighead carp are the most **threatening**. That's because each fish eats a lot of plankton each day. They compete with native species for this food source and often win.

Many native fish and mussels eat plankton as well. Without enough food, these native species' populations will decrease. **Ecosystems** will become unbalanced, leading to even more problems.

STAY ALERT

Asian carp are filter feeders. They gulp mouthfuls of water, straining the plankton out.

Asian carp reproduce more and grow faster than native fish. These fish end up eating too much of the plankton in an area, leaving less food for other species.

HEADING NORTH

Ever since they escaped from the fish farms in the southern United States, Asian carp have spread. They moved upstream in the Mississippi River through **locks**. Boats traveling along the river picked up young Asian carp or eggs and carried them to other bodies of water.

Scientists are worried that Asian carp will eventually reach the Great Lakes. The Great Lakes fishing industry makes billions of dollars each year. Asian carp could seriously harm the ecosystem and cost the industry a lot of money.

STAY ALERT

A group called the Great Lakes Commission has been studying the spread of Asian carp for years and working to keep these fish out of the Great Lakes.

If they reach Minnesota, Asian carp could threaten the resort and sport fishing industry there. By outcompeting other fish for food, Asian carp may reduce the populations of native fish like walleye and perch.

A SHOCKING SURPRISE

In 2002, the U.S. Army Corps of Engineers built the first electric **barriers** to keep Asian carp away from Lake Michigan. These barriers send small electric pulses into the water, which work to keep fish away.

Closing down the Chicago Sanitary and Ship Canal may be one way to stop Asian carp from entering the Great Lakes. However, this waterway is used for shipping, so closing it would mean lost jobs and money for the nearby area. Scientists are looking for other ways to stop their spread.

STAY ALERT

Some Asian carp have made it past the electric barriers. Grass carp have been found in the Great Lakes, but no silver or black carp have been found there.

The Chicago Sanitary and Ship Canal connects the Great Lakes to the Mississippi River. That's the waterway many people fear Asian carp will use to reach the Great Lakes.

SCIENTIFIC STUDIES

Scientists are looking for ways to stop the spread of Asian carp. One study says Asian carp stay away from water that has added gas in it, such as carbon dioxide. Other scientists are trying to find diseases or **chemicals** that can reduce Asian carp numbers.

Some of these plans might work. But before these plans go into effect, scientists must determine how they will impact other wildlife as well. Introducing chemicals or diseases could cause even more problems.

STAY ALERT

Scientists are testing new tools like sound barriers and air bubbles to keep Asian carp out of the Great Lakes. Experts think these types of barriers could stop most fish from getting through.

Adding carbon dioxide to water makes it bubbly like soda! Asian carp don't seem to like it.

STOP THOSE CARP!

Asian carp now live in more than 40 states. People have tried netting them, catching them, and trapping them, all with little success.

Instead of focusing on stopping the spread of Asian carp, some people want to simply make use of the overpopulation. One chef in Louisiana has figured out how to clean the fish well and wants to sell them for food. He calls the idea "Can't Beat 'Em. Eat 'Em." Some people even want to use carp as cat food or fertilizer!

STAY ALERT

Grass carp have spread the furthest. However, grass carp eat plants instead of plankton, so they are usually less threatening than silver and bighead carp.

Asian carp are large fish that have thrived in their new habitats and continue to invade new places. Where might they wind up next?

GLOSSARY

algae: plantlike living things that are mostly found in water

appetite: a wish to eat when food is present

barrier: something that makes traveling hard

chemical: matter added to other matter to cause changes

ecosystem: all the living things in an area

habitat: the natural place where an animal or plant lives

larvae: the early stage of some animals, before they grow into adults

lock: a device for raising and lowering ships between stretches of water that are different levels

plankton: a tiny plant or animal that floats in a body of water

reproduce: when an animal creates another creature just like itself

spawn: a way some marine animals reproduce in which eggs are let loose in the water

startle: to move or jump when scared or surprised

threatening: giving signs as something that could cause harm

FACT CHECK

1. There are ____________ species of invasive Asian carp in the United States.
   a. two b. three c. four

2. Bighead and silver carp eat __________.
   a. plants b. snails c. plankton

3. Asian carp can cause problems if they reach the __________.
   a. Great Lakes b. Mississippi River c. ocean

Answers: 1. c, 2. c, 3. a

ON THE INTERNET

Asian Carp

www.britannica.com/animal/Asian-carp

Read about the different species of Asian carp, then learn more about what's being done to help stop their spread.

Asian Carp

https://a-z-animals.com/animals/asian-carp/

Learn more about Asian carp, including where they live, what they eat, and more.

Publisher's note to educators and parents: Our editors have carefully reviewed these websites to ensure that they are suitable for students. Many websites change frequently, however, and we cannot guarantee that a site's future contents will continue to meet our high standards of quality and educational value. Be advised that students should be closely supervised whenever they access the Internet.

INDEX